# The Christmas Gift

A story told by Grandma Cookie

By: Brenda Anderson

**www.brendaskidsbooks.com**

**Printed in the United States of America**

Softcover Version:
ISBN - 13: 978-0-9965766-0-4
ISBN - 10: 099657660

Dedicated to my readers:

May you feel the light of Christ in your hearts
and strive to be like Him.


A Special Thanks:

To everyone who helped make this book possible.
For all of your support and help.
I love and appreciate you all.

Emmylou bounced around the barnyard excitedly. She could see the bright Christmas lights, that twinkled on the Christmas tree, in the window of the farm house.

"Ginger and Bella do you see all the lights?"
Emmylou bleated.

Ginger and Bella were also excited. They had been watching
The Farmer and his Wife hurry around the barnyard.
"Grandma Cookie what is The Farmer and his Wife doing?"
asked the kids.

"Come kids and I will answer that question by telling you the story of Christmas," invited Grandma Cookie.

"Christmas!" cheered the kids. The kids loved stories, they
hurried to listen.

"What is Christmas?" asked Miss Ellie.

"Christmas is the birthday of the Son of God," said Grandma
Cookie. "His name is Jesus Christ. Every year The Farmer and
his Wife make a stable scene for a Live Nativity. This helps
them remember the real meaning of Christmas. They invite
their family, friends, and neighbors to help them celebrate.
The fun part is, we get to help too." said Grandma Cookie.

Gus, the donkey, was listening as he hung his head over the fence. "I love this time of year. I get so excited because I get to help in the Christmas Nativity!" Gus exclaimed.

"Continue with the story of Jesus, Grandma Cookie," the
kids said happily. "We can't wait to hear!"

Grandma Cookie smiled as she continued to tell the story. "Every year The Farmer invites a person to read the story of when Jesus was born. They read the story from the Bible. I will tell you the way the story goes."

And it came to pass, the Roman Emperor commanded all of his people in the land to return to the cities where they were born, to pay taxes. Even though baby Jesus would soon be born, Joseph and Mary made the long trip to Bethlehem to pay their taxes.

When Joseph and Mary arrived in the city of Bethlehem they
tried to find a place to stay. Joseph went to all of the inns,
an inn is like a motel where people stay when they travel.
All of the inns were full. There was no where for them to
stay. They would have to stay in the stable where the
animals lived.

That night baby Jesus was born in the stable. Mary wrapped baby Jesus in snuggly warm clothes called swaddling clothes, and laid him in the manger.

The Manger was soft and cozy.  The manger had
hay in it for the animals to eat.

The angels were so happy baby Jesus was born.  They went to the hillside where the shepherds were watching their sheep.  Bright light shone all around the angels and the shepherds.  They were so afraid.  The angels said to the shepherds, "Fear not for behold we bring you tidings of great joy.  For unto you this day, baby Jesus, the Son of God is born.  You will find him in a manger wrapped in swaddling clothes."

When the angels left, the shepherds hurried to Bethlehem to see baby Jesus. They found him just as the angels had said, lying in a manger wrapped in swaddling clothes.

The wise men, who lived in the East, saw the new star.
They knew it meant baby Jesus was born. They traveled far
to see Jesus. The wise men brought Jesus precious gifts of
gold, frankincense, and myrrh.

When the wise men saw Jesus they knelt down to worship him. They gave Him the gifts that they had brought.

"This is my favorite part," Gus whispered softly. "The night is cold and the stars are twinkling brightly. The Farmer and his Wife and all of their friends and family sing Silent Night. It rings so beautifully through the still night air."

"So you see kids," sighed Grandma Cookie, "this is the reason The Farmer and his wife celebrate Christmas. It is a reminder to all of us that Jesus is the Gift. He is a gift from a loving Father in Heaven. God sent us his son Jesus, as a Savior, to help us so that someday we can return to live with him. The birth of Jesus is the reason they celebrate Christmas."

"Thank you Grandma Cookie!  We loved our Christmas story.  We will always try to remember the true meaning of Christmas.
**Jesus is the Gift.**"

*The End*

# The Farmers Wife - Brenda Anderson

I live on a farm in Idaho with my husband Shawn. One of my greatest joys in life is our grandchildren and children. I treasure the time I spend with each of them. My family is very important to me. I have always enjoyed family traditions and I strive to continue to establish them.

I Love Christmas!     One of my favorite Christmas traditions is our Live Nativity. We

have enjoyed this for years. Our first year we decided the Nativity would include just our family. Our Nativity plans grew very quickly when Shawn started to invite extended family, friends and neighbors. The night of our first Live Nativity the front yard was filled with people we love and enjoy spending time with.

One of the funniest  experiences we have had, is when Gus came up missing before Joseph and Mary had arrived. The show could not go on without him. Gus had been caught and tied up. When we went to get him for his part he had untied the knot on his lead rope and joined the other horses and mules in the pasture, a quarter of a mile away. Shawn and Sam found him and brought him home. We started about ten minutes late, but Gus was there.

We encourage everyone that attends to bring their children dressed up to participate. We do not have rehearsals, just a quick explanation of what the kids need to do. Most of the time we have kids out of place, and one of the animals may not stand still, but it doesn't matter. What is important is the message of The Nativity and the feelings we share.

I hope you will enjoy "The Christmas Gift". While it is a story for the Christmas Season, it is a message I hope you will carry with you in your heart all year.

More books written by
Brenda Anderson

The Farmers Wife Series:
Book 1 - Slippers for Hannah

Books also available as an ebook

Watch for more books to come.
www.Brendaskidsbooks.com

CPSIA information can be obtained at www.ICGtesting.com
Printed in the USA
LVOW02s2252170815

450471LV00006B/8/P

9 780996 576635